WHO
IS THE SCHOOL?

WHO
IS THE SCHOOL?

Photographs and Text by
Michael J. Sexton

THE WESTMINSTER PRESS
PHILADELPHIA

Published by The Westminster Press®
Philadelphia, Pennsylvania

PRINTED IN THE UNITED STATES OF AMERICA

Library of Congress Cataloging in Publication Data

Sexton, Michael J., 1939—
Who Is the School?

    1. Teaching—Pictorial works. I. Title.
LB1025.2.S4   371'.0022'2   72-13499
ISBN 0-664-20962-9

CONTENTS

FOREWORD

The only way I could create an in-depth photographic profile of a school was to become an "insider." For that reason I took a year off from graduate school at the University of Iowa to accept a job teaching in a "better," "typical" inner-city school in Denver, Colorado.

In the theme "Who Is the School?" I explain that the purpose of this study is to discover not merely what people do, but in essence who they are. The reader will, I hope, be able to see that "who they are" changes dramatically with the person's role in the school, the type of class or situation, the time of day, week, and year. Perhaps the big question is, Does one's self completely change because of the school environment—not merely one's role but his actual being?

The purpose of this study is not to give conclusion but rather to help the reader become involved with the people in a real school and study how each situation within the confines of that school affects "who they are." For example, it was brought to my attention that the "Visitors" sign, the grating on the windows, and so forth have very definite practical purposes. But my concern was with the composite effect these and other factors have upon individual people.

This project was conducted with a sincere attempt at complete honesty, and the school faculty and administration were told the exact nature and purpose of the study. I became firmly established as an "insider," and everyone became so used to seeing the camera that he became indifferent to it, almost as if it were part of me, an extra appendage. Neither flash nor strobe was used, for fear of interrupting the environment. Actually, my colleagues' openness allowed me to achieve such a level of intimacy that I could view an inside of the school rarely seen by anyone from the "outside" world. I encountered an unexpected and rather interesting disadvantage, however, in becoming so much a part of the school. Because of lack of detachment, I found it literally impossible to gain any kind of perspective of my work while I was in the midst of it. John Culkin has captured this frustration acutely: "We don't know who discovered water, but we're certain it wasn't a fish." Only later could I discern any real meaning from the pictures I had taken.

After much wrestling, I have concluded that it would be futile to try to attach *objective* significance to this kind of photographic study. What you see in this work (as in the case of all still photography) is not the real world. Everything you see is through the eye of the photographer, while at the same time you see it through your own eyes and through your own experience. It is the very nature of still photography to be subjective. Herein lies this medium's power: to freeze 1/60 of a second in time, to isolate one face from all the confusion of reality, to be able to study one expression. Yet, this aspect of photography is also its weakness. Whose face does the photographer select? Is that frozen split second truly representative of reality? The photographer must be aware of these questions and of his own subjectivity. The still photograph has a unique, intrinsic ability to convey a situation in a way that words and statistics cannot; but the still camera can, like no other instrument, turn people into things so they may be examined, scrutinized. Marshall McLuhan tells the story of an admiring friend who said to a proud mother, "My, that's a fine child you have there!" And she replied: "Oh, that's nothing. You should see his photograph."

For myself, I can only say: There were no secret cameras. There were no gimmicks or photographic trickery. I tried to be honest.

M.J.S.

THE SCHOOL

A big part of my world is a city school.
My school is a contemporary school.

My school exists in Denver, Colorado.
My school is not a ghetto school.
My school doesn't make the newspapers.
There are no headlines of racial dissent
  and rioting at my school.
My school was built in 1911.
My school is a contemporary school.

My school has a racial mixture of 66 percent white, 24 percent
  black, one busload of Chicanos.
My school has 800 students, 45 teachers.
My school is located in a middle-class neighborhood.
My school is jammed next to Colorado Boulevard.
Automobile traffic and ambulance sirens engulf my school.
My school is contemporary.

My school is surrounded by six "temporary" buildings—
  the first ones were built in 1919.
For over 50 years, the overflow of classes has been held
  in our "temporary" buildings.

The administration's solution some 20 years ago was to change
  the name from "temporaries" to "portables."
The students immediately started referring to them as "port-
  holes."
Last year, they changed the name of our six "portholes"
  to our "new outer buildings."
Our problem is solved.
My school is contemporary.

15

ARCHITECTURE: PENITENTIARY GOTHIC

18

One of the "temporary" buildings—53 years old

TWO WORLDS

"There is a world of difference between the modern home environment of integrated electric information and the classroom. Today's television child is attuned to up-to-the-minute 'adult' news—inflation, rioting, war, taxes, crime, bathing beauties—and is bewildered when he enters the nineteenth-century environment that still characterizes the educational establishment where information is scarce but ordered and structured by fragmented, classified patterns, subjects, and schedules."

—MARSHALL McLUHAN

Remember waiting in the nurse's office,
the room that always felt like something
from a Dickens novel?
It's still there

20

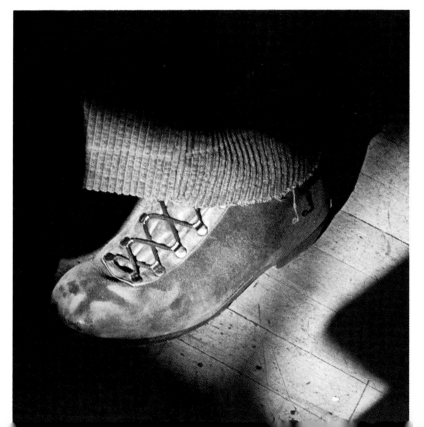

WHO
IS THE SCHOOL?

This study is an attempt to deal with people—not simply with what they do, but in essence who they are.

Look at us, feel us, become involved with us. We are the school.

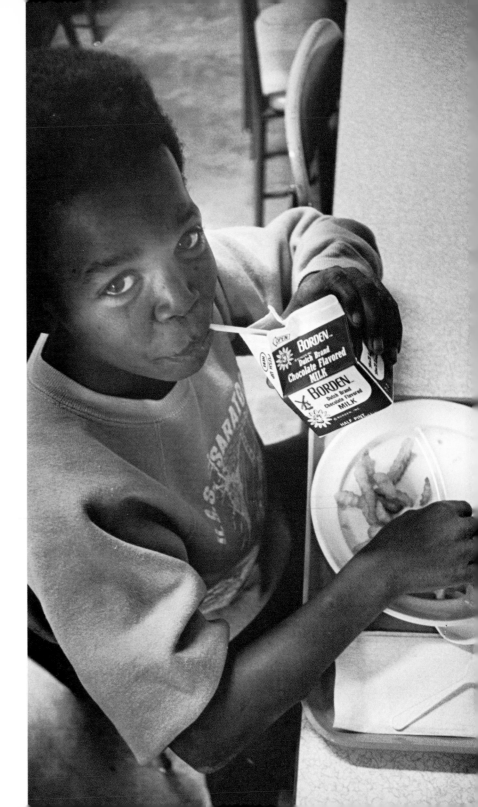

LIMITS OF
THE GOOD TEACHER

One of the great American myths that still persists is that some young energetic teacher can change the system. This fairy tale is perpetuated by television programs, the movies, and even in some college education classes. The naïve young teacher is quickly shocked into reality. First of all, like the junior senator, she has very little power to change the existing system. Secondly, no matter how dynamic and compassionate she is, she will still face the real world: teaching *five* classes a day, facing 180 real children, some of whom can't stand to look at her. Most of them she will never get to know.

After this initiation of fire, we hope that we are left with the good teacher: a person who, in spite of all the dirty looks and face-to-face confrontations, still loves children; a person who, despite all the indifference that surrounds her, and all her defeats, still persists in trying to teach with intensity.

And at the end of the week, exactly the same teachers,
    good teachers,
    are left only with complete physical exhaustion.
    Perhaps the big question is,
How long can the really good teacher remain good?

After how many years of this emotional, physical
    drain does the good teacher start to compromise?
After how many years of breaking up fights
    and watching study halls
    does a teacher's stamina begin to be chipped away?
After how many years of checking hall passes and the girls' lav
    does the teacher's interest in her subject begin to fade?
After how many years of checking the desk tops
    for dirty words
    and enduring the penetrating noise level
    of the cafeteria duty
    does the good teacher begin to surrender to the system?

This downhill evolution is inevitable.
    One has only to look at the "senior" members of the faculty

TRIBUTE TO THE GOOD TEACHER

It is very plain to see that these teachers are trying tremendously hard to communicate with their students. I was amazed that these people could come to school Monday morning late in the year with some kind of preparation—and at the end of the week still have some go left in them.

THE ACADEMIC CLASS: POLARIZATION

Perhaps the most striking aspect of this study was the *tremendous* amount of redundancy in photographing children in the academic classes. The academic class is one of extremes. As these photographs came to life in the darkroom, one thing became clear: I had photographed almost exclusively two expressions. The students were either intensely occupied or they were at the opposite pole, in a state of absolute boredom. One other fact became obvious: there was a definite correlation between the length of time a child spent in school and the increased degree of boredom inside the confines of the academic class.

"Soap and education are not as sudden as a massacre,
but they are more deadly in the long run."

—MARK TWAIN

I was accused of posing this picture.
When I asked why, I was told to read the text
at the student's fingertips

THOUGHTS
OF FREEDOM

In exposing some of the pitfalls of the academic classroom and the stress that this artificial environment places on our children, we cannot deny the extreme importance of academic pursuit. It is here that we develop and nurture man's most precious possession: his intelligence. This gift does not come easily. It does require intensity and self-discipline, but its reward is the highest, for without it man can never hope to be free. With his usual penetrating insight, Lloyd Williams states that among the most massive misconceptions in the American ideology is that freedom is essentially the absence of restraint.

In *Progressive Education at the Crossroads*, Boyd Bode corrected several of John Dewey's associates who assert that freedom is the condition of intelligence. He pointed out to them that the reverse is true: intelligence is a basic condition of freedom.

"The essence of freedom is intellectual. Freedom in a physical, economic, or political sense is a secondary mode of freedom. This is not to say that such freedom is unimportant or unrelated to intellectual freedom, but rather that freedom of

the mind takes precedence over other forms of freedom. . . . This means not merely freedom of choice but freedom to have a part in setting up the *possible* choices."

—LLOYD P. WILLIAMS
Philosopher
University of Oklahoma

34

"We are free not because of what we statically are,
but in so far as we are becoming different
from what we have been."

—JOHN DEWEY

HOME EC AND SHOP

There is a striking contrast between nonacademic classes and the atmosphere of the academic classroom. There exists here a feeling of relaxation, more comfortable rapport between student and teacher, and a fine sense of reward in seeing a finished product, one's own creation.

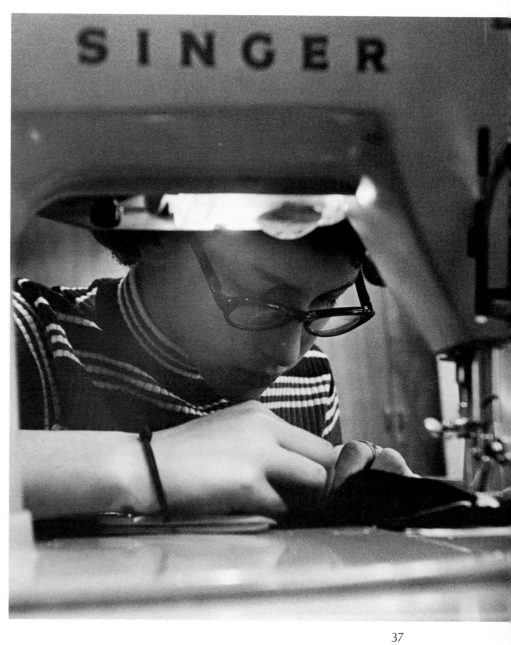

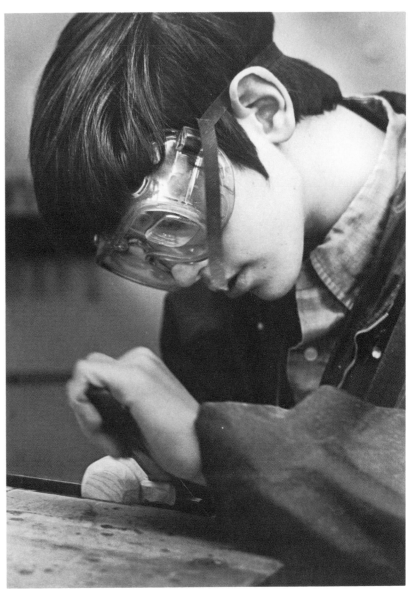

WHAT WE PLAY IS LANGUAGE. LISTEN!

Here one experiences a real sense of *Gemeinschaft,* the "we feeling," the sense of group accomplishment.

Yet, there is much more. These instruments are tools, used as language. They communicate . . . achievement, satisfaction, pride!

With all the clunkers and sour notes of a junior high school orchestra, the language of their instruments rings through: "We have accomplished something!"

"Things added to things, as statistics, civil history, are inventories. Things used as language are inexhaustively attractive!"

—RALPH WALDO EMERSON

THE MICROSCOPE

The two things a child will never forget about his junior high school science are the day he cut up the worm or frog and the day he first looked through the microscope. The microscope is a world of mystery! It is the mystery itself which becomes an unforgettable experience.

"The most beautiful thing we can experience is the mysterious. It is the source of all true art and science."

—ALBERT EINSTEIN, *October, 1930*

TEACHER ... TEACHER

On the very edge of his seat, a student is pleading for recognition. "Oh, teacher . . . *me* teacher!" His hand is stretched for what seems like minutes; then the teacher finally calls on someone else! That penetrating sting of defeat!

REALITY
OF EDUCATION

"The child is a reality; education must become a reality. But what does the 'development of the creative powers' mean? Is that the *reality* of education?"

—MARTIN BUBER

Precisely the same teacher who talks about creativity and innovation in October speaks of controlling children in January. "Let's get those damn kids out of the hallways!" This is reality!

The student who is refreshed and eager in September is enduring in March. This is reality!

The administrator who listens attentively in November is struggling for survival in May. This is reality!

The fresh new teacher from Kansas who is frightened by the black kids and repulsed by four-letter words decides to quit teaching. *This* is reality, Mr. Buber!

A "slow learner" is kept occupied with busywork

The involuntary muscles
    finally submit to a great yawn!

A teacher at the end of the day
    is with her Coke bottle—that great American symbol.
    And when that's dry, baby, there's nothing left!

49

AUTHORITY—
THE BEDROCK
OF THE SCHOOL

VISITORS

Section 824.2 of the
Revised Municipal Code prohibits
persons not having lawful business
in this school from being
in this building.

All visitors are required to report
directly to the main office for
permission to visit.

BY ORDER OF THE SUPERINTENDENT
DENVER PUBLIC SCHOOLS

*"From this arises the question
    whether it is better to be loved than feared,
    or feared rather than loved. It might
    perhaps be answered that we should wish to be both;
    but since love and fear can hardly exist together,
    if we must choose between them
    it is far safer to be feared than loved."*

—MACHIAVELLI

Yes, this is the principal's office!

I call this the assistant principal stare.
  He's the disciplinarian.
  Eighty percent of his job was just that look,
  and he used it to perfection.
  With that stare, he just controlled people. In fact,
  there were many moments when he was quite human
  and understanding.
  But he had that look
  which could put people in their place,
  and it was a very effective tool in his job

In essence, we are dealing with the polarization
    of control vs. innovation,
    similar to Machiavelli's dichotomy of love vs. fear.
    However,
    there must remain a system of checks and balances.
    The problem in the school is that at some point
    in the development of the organization
    this system of checks and balances became
    horribly distorted in favor of control.

"Bureaucracy is the sworn enemy of individual liberty,
    and of all bold initiative in matters of internal policy. . . .
    We may even say that the more conspicuously
    a bureaucracy is distinguished by its zeal,
    by its sense of duty, and by its devotion,
    the more also will it show itself to be petty, narrow,
    rigid, and illiberal."

—ROBERT MICHAELS

This is the Girls' Dean.
   She is trying to exert her authority
   with the greatest sensitivity

WHY?

The naïveness of the '50s is gone forever. Modern curricula in education stressed over and over again: "Ask questions! Be inquisitive! Ask why!" Then administrative orders were passed down to the students: "Get your hair cut!" "Dress properly!" "Respect your teachers!" They asked why.

With their newfound ability to question, both students and teachers demand a more autonomous role in the school. Will the modern school administrator somehow be willing to delegate some of his authority to teachers and students so they will be truly involved in the decision-making process? Can he afford not to?

Herein lies the frustrating paradox: The modern administrator can and should delegate authority, but how can he delegate *responsibility?* "Ah, there's the rub!" Do we invite "outsiders" to a school dance? If these "outsiders" cause a fight or a riot, who then accepts the responsibility? Is there any existing mechanism by which students and teachers, with all their newfound autonomy, can accept the full responsibility for their administrative decisions? Or do we resort to some kind of compromise, modern administrative trickery to make the masses feel relevant? "We'll set up a committee to look into it." In the meantime, the administrator has already made his decision.

As the faculty meeting moves along
    to new and exciting highs,
        the head counselor meticulously examines each movement
    of a fly as it moves across the desk top

As I scanned the faculty meeting,
    I finally found a face that was listening.
    But a closer look at her eyes revealed
    this senior faculty member had mastered the art
    of appearing attentive

59

THE DRESS CODE

After many long, long faculty meetings of exhausting debate, there is no longer a dress code.

And life goes on.

Someone asked me,
  "Why do so many of the black children
    still have their coats on in the classroom?"

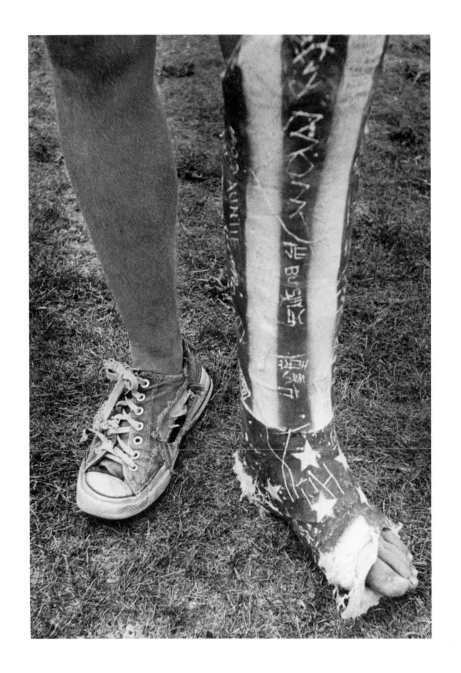

Ninth-grade boy!

61

ASSOCIATING TOGETHER

The greatest attribute the public school has over any other form of education is its potential for association.

"Among the laws that rule human societies there is one which seems to be more precise and clear than all others. If men are to remain civilized or to become so, the act of associating together must grow and improve in the same ratio in which the equality of conditions is increased."

—ALEXIS de TOCQUEVILLE

EQUAL EDUCATION: ABSURD

"Education is only the image and reflection of society. It imitates and reproduces the latter in abbreviated form; it does not create it. The evil is moral and deep-seated, and to expect education, which, after all, has but a part of each of its students, and for but a short time, to overcome deficiencies in the whole social order is absurd."

—ÉMILE DURKHEIM

In sharp contrast,
    this student, with his leather coat still on,
    sits uncomfortably,
    tensely grasping a pencil in his hand.
His folder on the desk top is soiled and wrinkled.
His effort is every bit as great as hers,
    as he strains to do his work.
How, then, can these two students be evaluated equally?

Observe the meticulous hair style, dress, penmanship,
    neat folder, and posture.
This student is the Puritan ethic.
She has been carefully groomed to function
    within the artificial confines of the classroom

THE CHICANOS

SOCIAL WORKER

These are the Chicanos. They represent one busload of "outsiders." Some teachers and administrators tried to make them feel as though they belonged. They clearly remained the "outsiders."

In describing "the others," Marshall McLuhan, in his usual style, wrote:
"The shock of recognition! In an electronic information environment, minority groups can no longer be contained—ignored. Too many people know too much about each other. Our new environment compels commitment and participation. We have become irrevocably involved with, and responsible for, each other."

All this sounds very hopeful, but the hard fact persists: these Chicano children remained "the others." Upon seeing these pictures, many teachers and students seemed queasy and uncomfortable. One teacher commented: "Oh, please, Mike, do you have to show these pictures? This is not our school!"

66

These children are real. They exist!

Albert Speer (Adolf Hitler's Minister of Armaments),
    after being released following twenty years at Spandau,
    confessed:
"If I had continued to see them as human beings,
    I could not have remained a Nazi.
    I did not hate them;
    I was indifferent to them.
    My crime was far worse because I was not an anti-Semite."

In spite of all of Marshall McLuhan's optimistic claims
    for the changes
    in our modern "electronic information environment,"
    this old wretched indifference still persists and thrives:
"I have lived in Chicago all my life and I still say
    we have no ghettos in Chicago."
                                    —RICHARD J. DALEY, June 8, 1963

"We hope by the end of 1967
    we will have removed every slum and blight home in
    Chicago."
                                    —RICHARD J. DALEY, May 18, 1967

"I know we haven't cleaned up all the slums,
    but I didn't create the slums, did I?"
                                    —RICHARD J. DALEY, September 3, 1968

67

HAPPY FACES

One of the faculty members kept asking me: "Where are the happy pictures? Where are the smiling faces?" As I scanned through my thousands of negatives, I discovered many happy pictures. There was only one problem: they were all taken outside the classroom.

There is another rather dramatic consistency in these pictures. Although the different racial and economic groups were mixed and seemed to get along in the controlled classroom atmosphere, in literally every picture I had taken of situations where the students could group themselves (play yard, cafeteria, and after school), I found no racial mingling. Is this integration?

PHYSICAL EDUCATION

The air still hangs heavy with the smell of sweat and sweat socks. In an instant the mind flashes back to one's own gym class experience: running, sucking up thick, moist air through the nostrils.

Here there is no sense of the '70s. It's like reverting back in time. All remains the same. The kids still push and shove; the whistle of the gym teacher still shrieks and bounces off the walls. Boys are exploding with energy, releasing the surge of aggression built up during many confined hours in the classroom. The whole atmosphere is almost as if it were in a time capsule, sealed tight for twenty years. Nothing is changed.

Touch me—In our visual electronic world,
touch has become something to be avoided.
In an alien environment of the institution
one human being reaches out to touch another.
Communicate!

THE MATH TEACHER

Math is the black-and-white subject. Either the answer is comfortably clear or the student remains in some kind of stupefying limbo of confusion. Unlike history, English, and shop, a student cannot grasp partial understanding of math. There are no shades of gray.

Here the thin threads of communication between teacher and student are stressed to the limit. The teacher is in a frustrating role of trying to make something that is "absolute" and "unqualified" comprehendible to a student. The student can only long to be somewhere else.

Is it the innate nature of this subject which causes so much anguish in the communicative process?

"Thus mathematics may be defined as the subject in which we never know what we are talking about, nor whether what we are saying is true."

—BERTRAND RUSSELL

THEY'RE
STILL CHILDREN

A teacher comments, when he first sees these pictures of ninth-grade students in his own class: "My God, they're still children! With all the hustle, we sometimes forget that they're still—children."

"A father sees a son nearing manhood.
What shall he tell that son?
'Life is hard; be steel; be a rock.'
And this might stand him for the storms
And serve him for humdrum and monotony
And guide him amid sudden betrayals
And tighten him for slack moments.
'Life is a soft loam; be gentle; go easy.'"

—CARL SANDBURG

GIRLS' GYMNASTICS

Prepubescence has become synonymous with awkwardness.

And yet, in the spindly form of a thirteen-year-old girl there is a strange kind of grace.

THE FACULTY LOUNGE

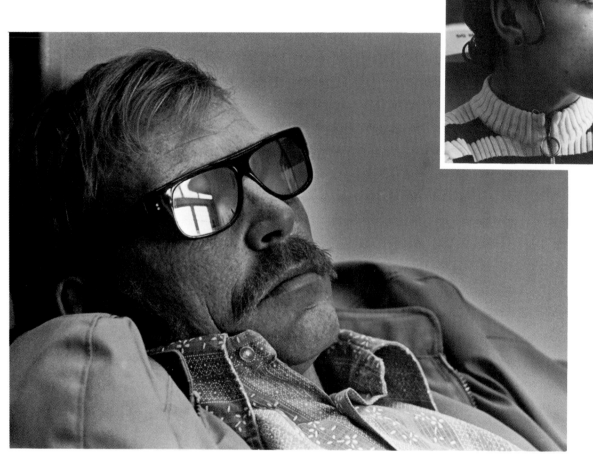

It's February. . . .

It's eighth period. . . .

It's Friday!

FIELD DAY

Field day is the one day of the year spent out of doors. It's late in May. There is a feeling of great excitement, and anticipation of the games. "We have survived another school year!" All inhibitions are cast aside.

On this day,
  even senior faculty members "let it all hang out"

"Nothing else in this song—only your face.
    Nothing else here—
    only your drinking, night-gray eyes."

            —CARL SANDBURG

WINDOWS

AND YET,
THE CHILD REMAINS
ELUSIVE

When all is said, there is much cause for hope. The face of a child . . .

"I wanted a man's face looking into the jaws and
Throat of life with something proud on his face,
So proud no smash of the jaws,
No gulp of the throat leaves the face in the end
With anything else than the old proud look."

—CARL SANDBURG